IMAGES
of Rail

TOLEDO TROLLEYS

IMAGES
of Rail

TOLEDO TROLLEYS

Kirk F. Hise and Edward J. Pulhuj

ARCADIA
PUBLISHING

Published by Arcadia Publishing
Charleston, South Carolina

Library of Congress Catalog Card Number: 2006927305

For all general information contact Arcadia Publishing at:
Telephone 843-853-2070
Fax 843-853-0044
E-mail sales@arcadiapublishing.com
For customer service and orders:
Toll-Free 1-888-313-2665

Visit us on the Internet at www.arcadiapublishing.com

CONTENTS

ACKNOWLEDGMENTS

The authors would like to thank all people who took the time to capture and preserve a piece of Toledo streetcar and interurban history. This book would not have been possible without their contributions. It is dedicated to all of them.

INTRODUCTION

Early horsecars were nice in good weather but difficult to drive in bad weather. They were four-wheeled cars with one horsepower, and the motorman stood on the front platform with little or no protection. The electric cars were like the horsecars in design at first. Gradually the cars were enlarged and more enclosed, as their composition advanced from wood to steel.

In 1916, Toledo received an order of 60 steel cars from Kuhlman Car Company of Cleveland, numbered 801 to 860. These cars became the mainstay of the Community Traction Company (CTC). All the earlier cars were gone by 1941 except a few, which had been converted to use as work trains.

In 1931, eight double-end cars 39 feet long with 44 seats were purchased from Durham, South Carolina. Numbered 901 through 908, they operated on lines that had been cut back so that they had no turning facilities. They were also used in rush-hour service and on lighter traveled lines. Some of the 800s suffered wrecks and were not returned to service.

As car lines were abandoned and converted to bus operations, there was an excess of cars. In 1942, 23 of the 800s were sold to Birmingham, Alabama, for wartime use where they ran out their days.

In December 1949, the last car line in Toledo, the Long Belt was abandoned, and all remaining cars were scrapped at the Central Avenue barns. Two car bodies were sold, and they are gone now. The private car "Toledo" survives at the Trolleyville USA museum near Cleveland. Car No. 582 is at the Northern Ohio Trolley Museum near Chippewa Lake. Tarta replaced the CTC in 1971, and it continues bus transportation today on many routes that began in the trolley days.

One

EARLY TOLEDO STREETCARS

This c. 1874 photograph shows a one-horse sleigh with two boys in it and, in the background, Monroe Street horsecar No. 104. The Monroe Street line ran out Monroe Street to Auburn Avenue to Woodlawn Cemetery. (Courtesy of the F. D. Cairns collection.)

Adams Street line car No. 463 carries a U.S. mail sign in this c. 1900 photograph.

Toledo Consolidated Street Railway Company car No. 16 is seen here in this *c.* 1895 photograph at Monroe and Adams Streets. (Courtesy of the Jim Teal collection.)

The *c.* 1897 photograph of this Oak Street car on Summit Street at St. Clair Street is from a Lake Erie Park and Casino brochure.

Toledo Traction car No. 157 is at the casino on the Summit-Broadway line. The casino burned soon after this *c.* 1895 photograph was taken. (Courtesy of the Jim Teal collection.)

This Toledo Electric Street Railway car is on the South Street–Union Depot line in this *c.* 1895 photograph. (Courtesy of the Jim Teal collection.)

These two cars are at Cherry Street at Canton Avenue on the Lagrange and Maumee lines in this c. 1900 photograph. (Courtesy of the R. Hubbard collection.)

Toledo Electric Street Railway car No. 312 is seen here by the Canton Avenue barn in this c. 1890 photograph. Car No. 312 was said to be a fast car. The Canton Avenue carbarn burned on January 19, 1891, and the company lost 27 motorcars. The company had just built a new carbarn at Ontario and Galena Streets.

Here is the Toledo Traction Company carbarn at Monroe and Summit Streets in this *c.* 1900 photograph. This building later became the Pennsylvania Railroad freight house.

The former interurban station and Hagerty's Bowling Alley can be seen in the background of this c. 1943 photograph of Community Traction Company (CTC) car No. 834 on the Cherry Street line at Superior and Adams Streets. (Courtesy of the H. Haack collection.)

15

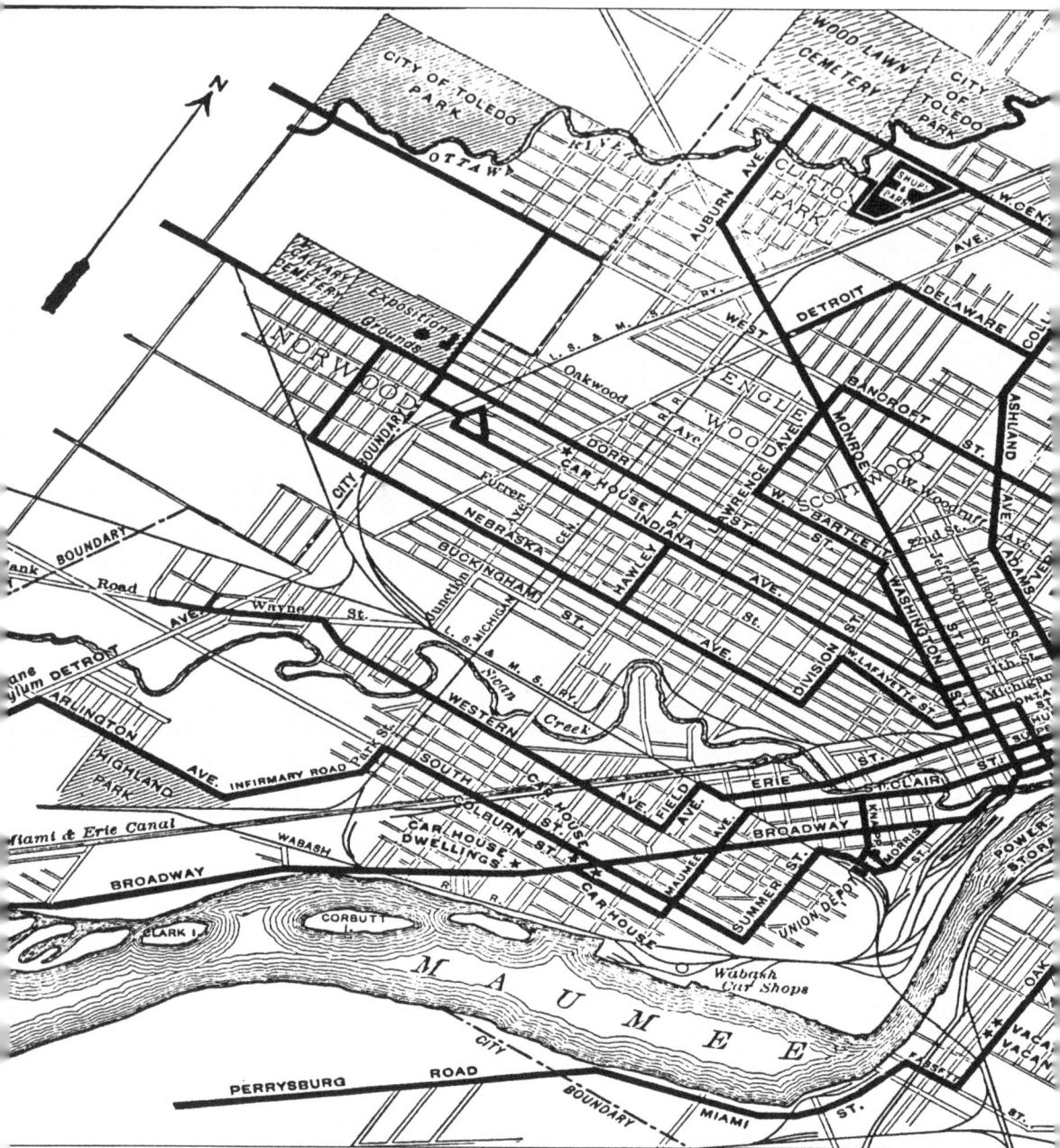

This map shows many of the different streetcar lines that were in operation about 1911. From the information supplied on the previous pages, one is able to see how the different lines helped

TOLEDO RAILWAYS
LIGHT COMPANY LINES
TOLEDO, OHIO.

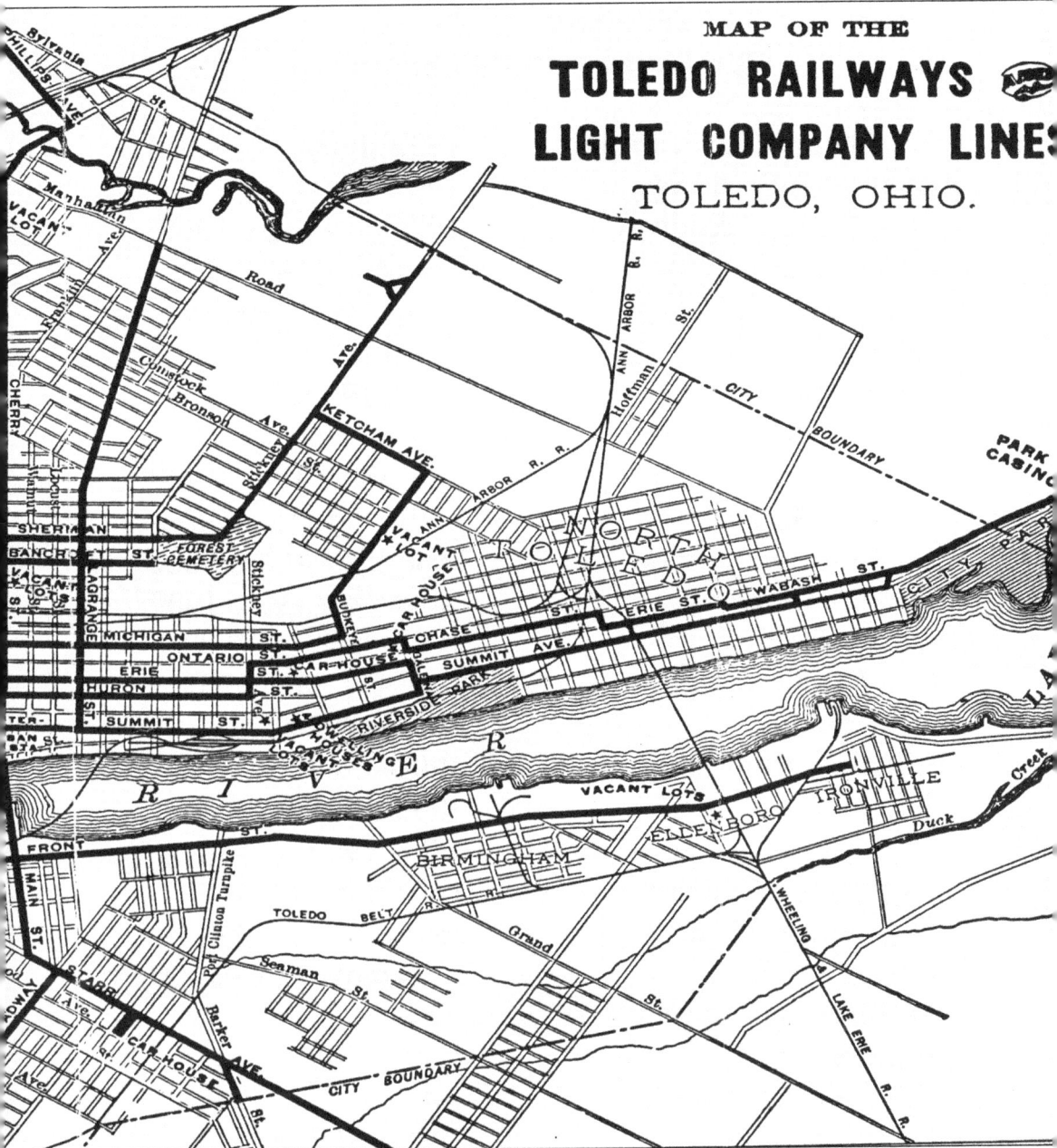

Toledo to grow and develop into the city that it is today.

Toledo Streetcar Lines
Operating From 1902 to 1909

Broadway & Lower Summit	1902–1904
Summit & Broadway	1905 –1909
Dorr & East Broadway	1902 –February 1905
East Broadway	March 1905–1909
Dorr	March 1905–1909
Long Belt	1902–1909
Short Belt	1902–1909
Erie & Nebraska	1902–October 1903
Nebraska & Lagrange	November 1903–1909
Western & Oak	1902–June 15, 1903
Western Avenue	June 15, 1903–October, 1903
Western& Erie	November 1903–1909
Union Depot	1902–June 15, 1903
Oak & Union Depot	June 15, 1903–1909
Ironville	1902–1909
Cherry & Union Depot	1902–1909
Glassboro	1902–1903
Michigan	1904–1909
Lagrange & Colburn	1902–June 1903
Lagrange & Maumee	July 1903–October 1903
Maumee & Starr	November 1903–1909
Indiana & Forest Cemetery	1902–1905
Indiana	1906–1908
Indiana & Stickney	1909
Huron & South	1902–1909
Bancroft Belt	1902–1909
Lagrange Short Line	December 1903–1909

The information presented here shows many of the different streetcar lines that carried passengers to and from their destinations around Toledo.

Toledo Railway and Light Company (TRY&L) car No. 125 is seen here at the Dorr Street barns. This *c.* 1910 photograph may have been taken near shift change, as there are so many of the crewmen in the photograph.

Here is TRY&L car No. 144 at the Central Avenue carbarns. The Long Belt line ran from Summit Street, out Adams Street to Ashland Avenue; west, crossing Bancroft Street to Collingwood Avenue; west at Central Avenue to Auburn Avenue; and on to Monroe Street to Summit Street. Cars ran both ways on the Long Belt.

At the end of the Broadway line, TRY&L car No. 170 can be seen in this *c.* 1910 photograph. The Summit-Broadway line and Point Place line ran from a loop at Glendale Avenue, Broadway Street to downtown, and on north on Summit Street to Bay View Park in North Toledo. The Point Place line started here and ran to Point Place, turning on 121st Street north to Edgewater Drive. The Toledo Beach line went out on the Point Place line also, going across the Ottawa River at 131st Street and continuing north to Toledo Beach until 1927.

For some unknown reason, TRY&L car No. 206 is loaded on a truck trailer in this photograph taken around 1902.

Here TRY&L car No. 207 sits at the Central Avenue barns. It was a single-truck, double-end car and had a city service emblem on its side. This photograph was taken before 1921, during TRY&L ownership, before the formation of the CTC. This car was built in 1897 by Barney and Smith and was later rebuilt with doors. The sign on the left side door reads, "Passengers Pay on Leaving."

Seen in this *c.* 1901 photograph is TRY&L car No. 301 at the end of the Ironville line at Front and Millard Avenues. This car would have stopped at the Ohio Central Railroad station on Main Street. The fender sign advertises night school starting on October 1, 1901.

The heavy bar hanging on the side of TRY&L car No. 304, seen here at the Dorr Street barn, is for the emergency towing of another trolley. The Dorr Street line ran south on Monroe Street, west to Eleventh Street, to Washington Street out Washing Street to Dorr Street, to Fairlawn Avenue and the New York Central Railroad where a wye was located. It returned to downtown on the same route. This photograph was taken around 1908.

The rail line in the background of this c. 1910 photograph of TRY&L car No. 302 could place it at the west end of the Nebraska line at the Lake Shore and Michigan Southern Railroad. Later this rail line would become the New York Central Railroad. The Nebraska-Lagrange line ran from the loop at Brown Avenue on Nebraska Avenue into downtown; to Division Street to Avondale Street, to Lafayette Street; on Lafayette to Ontario Street to Monroe Street, to Superior Street, to Cherry Street; out Cherry Street to East Bancroft Street; and east to Lagrange Street, out Lagrange Street to Manhattan Boulevard to a turnaround loop at the end of the line.

This c. 1908 photograph of TRY&L car No. 309 on the Summit-Broadway Street line was taken during the Grand Army of the Republic convention held in Toledo.

The intersection of Summit, Cherry, and St. Clair Streets was a very busy place in trolley days. Broadway-Summit cars went out Summit, Cherry cars turned north on Cherry Street, and Starr Avenue and East Broadway Street cars turned south over the Cherry Street bridge. Interurban cars, Lake Shore Electric (LSE), Ohio Public Service (OPS), Toledo, Fostoria and Findlay (TF&F), and the Maumee Valley cars all passed through this area. Marvin Hardy and his father were switch tenders here. They were busy throwing track switches for cars going in different directions. There were inbound cars as well as the outbound ones. According to Hardy, a car crew only got mad at him one time. He threw a switch wrong, and the car ran past a ways before realizing the mistake. Then it had to back up in all that traffic, to get headed the right way.

This postcard shows the St. Clair Street and Summit Street intersection.

TRY&L car No. 325 is at the intersection of Summit, Cherry, and St. Clair Streets in this *c.* 1925 photograph.

The Nebraska-Lagrange line, seen here with TRY&L car No. 310, was said to run "pole" because of the people living at each end of the line in those days. This photograph was taken around 1910. (Courtesy of the W. E. Hague collection.)

Here is a c. 1910 photograph of TRY&L car No. 339, also on the Nebraska-Lagrange line. (Courtesy of the F. D. Cairns collection.)

The Dorr Street barns were located at the corner of Dorr Street and Detroit Avenue. This c. 1910 photograph shows TRY&L car No. 343 and a number of motormen and conductors who worked the TRY&L.

Toledo Traction car No. 399 used to run on the Erie and Nebraska route but was taken off the roster by 1917.

This photograph of TRY&L car No. 403 on East Broadway Street at Earl Street shows Ed Davis on the left and Daniel Willmont in the fur coat. Willmont worked for the CTC for many years. He passed away in 1963.

The Cherry Street bridge was still under construction when this *c.* 1913 photograph of TRY&L car No. 404 on the Oak line on was taken. The Oak Street line started on Madison Avenue and Summit Street to Cherry Street, right on Cherry Street across the bridge to Front Street, west to Oak Street, and south on Oak to Fassett Street to Miami Street. At Miami Street and Oakdale Street, it passed the Baltimore and Ohio Railroad coal and ore docks. On Miami Street it went into Rossford Street to Bangor Street, which was the end of the line. The Maumee Valley cars had continued on through Rossford along the River Road to Perrysburg. There the Maumee Valley crossed over the Maumee River and back to Toledo along the river, joining the Broadway car line into downtown. Cars ran both directions on the valley line. The Maumee Valley line was abandoned on October 13, 1924. The route was replaced by buses. At Maumee, the Toledo, Waterville and Southern (TW&S) connected and ran out to Waterville in 1901. It ran until 1914. The TW&S was damaged many times by ice floes, and the company gave up trying to replace the track. (Courtesy of the W. E. Hague collection.)

Car No. 419 was built by TRY&L in 1899 from two small car bodies. They were on maximum traction trucks and were 39 feet, 3 inches long. (Courtesy of the F. D. Cairns collection.)

This photograph was taken after TRY&L car No. 419 was rebuilt with Brill trucks. The Union Station South line started at Monroe and Summit Streets to Knapp Street to the Union Depot; on Emerald Street to Summit Street to South Avenue West on South Avenue, crossing the Nickel Plate Railroad, the Miami and Erie Canal, the Ohio Electric Railway, and the Michigan Central Railroad to Spencer Street; and left on Spencer to Arlington Street to Detroit Avenue and the old Toledo State Hospital. The Toledo, Bowling Green and Southern had used this route from Arlington to downtown Toledo.

Sitting here at Starr Avenue barns, TRY&L car No. 432 is carrying an Ironville sign, as Ironville cars ran out of this barn. This photograph was taken around 1910. (Courtesy of the W. E. Hague collection.)

Track work is being completed at Collingwood Avenue and Delaware Street in this view looking toward downtown Toledo. (Courtesy of the Willard Edson collection.)

TRY&L car No. 449 is seen in this *c.* 1910 photograph at the Toledo and Western Railroad (T&W) station in West Toledo at the Point. The Cherry Street line ran from Summit and Cherry Streets; out Cherry Street to Collingwood Avenue (the Stickney line crossed at East Bancroft Street); continuing on Collingwood to Detroit Avenue; to Phillips Avenue, west on Sylvania Avenue to Tremainsville Road and the new Point; and out Tremainsville to Thrush Street and a wye turnaround. The T&W met this line until 1936 along Tremainsville Road for its entrance into Toledo. (Courtesy of the F. D. Cairns collection.)

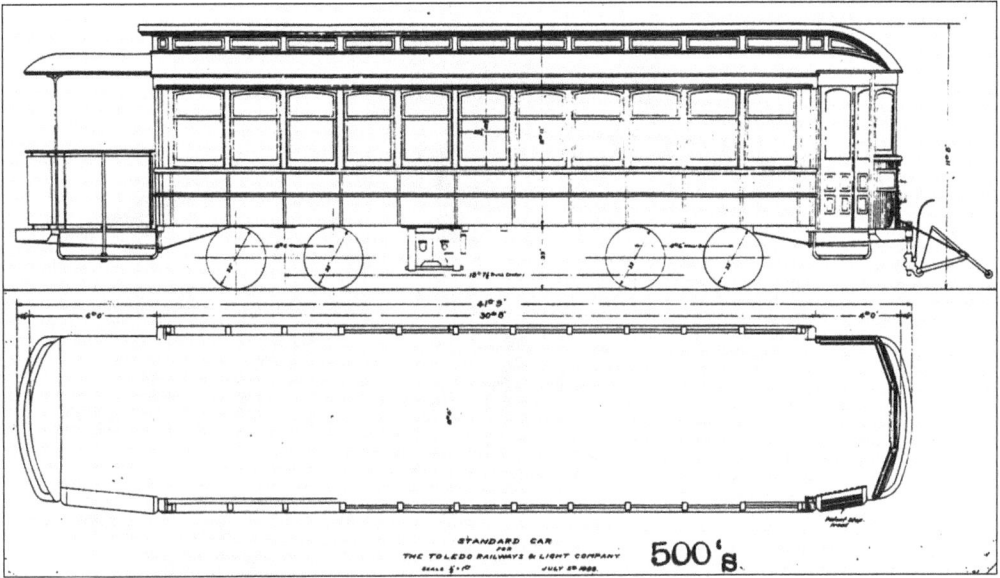

STANDARD CAR
FOR
THE TOLEDO RAILWAYS & LIGHT COMPANY
SCALE ½"=1'   JULY 29 1909.
500's.

This diagram is for TRY&L 500-series cars as originally built in 1909. High-number cars in the series above 550 were geared for about 50 miles per hour. They were regularly used on the Toledo Beach line. Also, many of them carried air whistles. Some of these cars were rebuilt into the 700 series.

This *c.* 1910 photograph of TRY&L car No. 587 was taken at the Kuhlman plant in Cleveland.

On the Nebraska-Lagrange line, TRY&L car No. 512 had its roof rebuilt and the trucks changed. This photograph was taken around 1910.

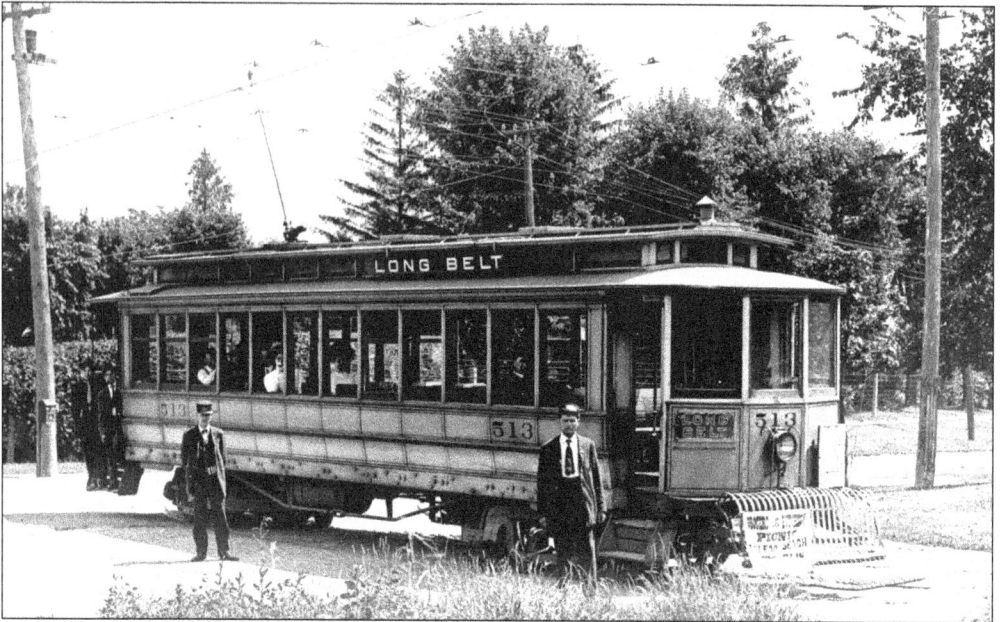

TRY&L car No. 513 on the Long Belt line has a sign that reads, "This car for White City." The sign on the fender reads, "About Toledo Beach Picnic." This photograph was taken around 1910.

TRY&L car No. 525 is seen here on the Erie and Western route in this *c.* 1907 photograph. The Erie Street line ran north on Superior Street past the interurban station at Jackson Street to Cherry Street, west to Erie Street, and north to Galena Street to the end of the line. The Western line ran south on Summit Street to Monroe Street, west to St. Clair Street, south to Emerald Street and west to Field Street, and south to Western Street, crossing the Nickel Plate Railroad, Miami and Erie Canal, and Lima-Toledo Railway, then crossing the Michigan Central Railroad to Wayne Street and then west to Hanover Street to the end of the line.

Sitting at the carbarn on Galena Street, TRY&L car No. 542 was a Summit-Broadway car. The conductor was Curtis Cousino, and the motorman was Jim Klotz. This c. 1908 postcard was given to author Kirk F. Hise by Star Taylor, a retired Toledo Beach dispatcher. (Courtesy of the Kirk F. Hise collection.)

This photograph was taken around 1915. The destination sign on TRY&L car No. 563 at the Starr Avenue barns reads, "East Broadway." The Starr Avenue line ran from Cherry Street to Superior Street to Jefferson Avenue to Summit Street to Cherry Street. It crossed the Cherry Street bridge to Main Street to Starr, crossing east. The Toledo Belt Railway ran from the Wheeling and Lake Erie Railroad to Dearborn Avenue, right on Dearborn to Dover Place, and then back to Starr and downtown. The OPS came along the north side of Starr Avenue and crossed the Toledo Terminal Railroad. It then joined the Starr Avenue line west of the crossing. On the north side of Starr Avenue, there was a loop just west of the Toledo Terminal Railroad in a field. When the Starr Avenue line was abandoned in 1939, the OPS cut back before the Toledo Terminal crossing at Ryan station and discontinued its passenger service. (Courtesy of the Joe Galloway collection.)

The Short Belt line ran out Monroe Street to Detroit Avenue, right on Detroit to Delaware Street, and then to Adams Street with the Long Belt line to Summit Street. Cars ran both directions on the Short Belt line. Pictured here is TRY&L car No. 564 on the Short Belt line. This photograph was taken around 1908.

A 500-series car on Central Avenue at the New York Central crossing is seen in this August 18, 1909, photograph before the viaduct was built. (Courtesy of the Kirk F. Hise collection.)

The rear vestibule has been enclosed on TRY&L car No. 592, which is seen here around 1910 on the lead track at the Central Avenue barns.

CTC car No. 610 is seen here around 1940 at the Central Avenue barns.

This *c.* 1938 photograph of CTC car No. 611 at the Starr Avenue barns was taken just before the abandonment of the Starr line.

The Bancroft Belt line ran out Adams Street to Michigan Street, to Canton north, to Woodruff Avenue west to Vermont Street, north to Bancroft Street, and west to Ashland Avenue, joining the Long Belt line. Then it went on Lawrence Avenue south to Washington Street and on to Madison Avenue and Superior Street. Cars ran both directions on the Bancroft Belt line. CTC car No. 635 is seen here around 1917 on the line. (Courtesy of the F. D. Cairns collection.)

CTC car No. 634 at the Central Avenue barns in 1941 is being scrapped. (Courtesy of the H. Haack collection.)

This photograph shows where CTC car No. 657 hit a tree on Collingwood Avenue. This photograph was taken around 1920.

Sixty new cars are being rapidly completed for the Toledo Railway & Light Co. by the G. C. Kuhlman of Cleveland. These cars are of all shell construction and have an overall length of fifty feet. The front half of the car is arranged for longitudinal seats and the rear half for transverse seats. Passengers are loaded at the front end through an entrance which is 56 inches wide and discharge from the center through two exit doors. Collection is made from the passengers as they pass the conductor at the center of the car going to the rear of the car,, or leaving. This scheme makes it possible to load the front half of the car without making collections and has the very great advantage of quick loading.

White enameled stanchions are used at the entrance and exit which properly divide the streams of passengers. The head lining of the car is also white enameled, which give a very attractive and sanitary appearance to the car.

These cars are mounted on Brill Type 51E trucks, having a wheel base of 4 ft. 10 inches. The wheel diameter is 26 inches and the distance between truck centers is 25 feet. Each truck is equipped with one Westinghouse 515 B1 motor rated 40hp Type HL Westinghouse Control is used and Tomlinson Automatic Couplers are provided which make it possible to run the cars in two car trains during rush hour service. Peter Smith Forced Draft heaters are used for heating and ventilating the cars and the fresh air is taken in from the side rather than from underneath the car which insures pure air being driven into the car and gives a very positive ventilation during the heating season.

Westinghouse Air Breaks are used and are arranged to permit the operation of one, tow or three car trains. The emergency position of the braking valve is arranged to automatically apply sand to the rail.

National Pneumatic Door Operating Mechanisms are used and each door is controlled by an air engine. The front door can be operated either by the motorman from his position in front or by the conductor from his position in the center of the car. This makes it possible for the conductor to open the front door on trail cars at congested traffic points. The center doors are controlled entirely by the conductor.

The power circuit on each car is run through the door mechanism and it si not possible to start the car until all doors have been closed. Opening a door automatically breaks the power circuit. Controls are provided with dead-man control which automatically cuts off the power and applies the brake in case anything disables the motorman.

As a "Safety First" feature, the floor mats are laid transversely instead of longitudinally, with the idea of preventing slipping accidents within the car. Lintern car signal systems is used which indicates by tail-lights whether or not power is being applied to the car and makes it possible for following cars to keep a safe distance.

The weight of the car complete is 18 tons.

The seating capacity of the car is 56 passengers.

This memorandum describes and outlines the features of a new line of Toledo cars numbered 800 to 860. It was compiled by Kirk F. Hise.

This builder's photograph of CTC car No. 801 was taken at the Kuhlman plant in Cleveland around 1916.

CTC car No. 803 is seen here at the Central Avenue barns.

This photograph shows CTC car No. 803 with a new fender and couplers.

The first car back in Toledo after the strike at the casino was CTC car No. 804. This photograph was taken around 1919.

Fred J. Young Frank W. Wiley Mayor Start Charles H. Forsgard

The caption under this photograph published in a local newspaper read, "A special ceremony last night marked the final run of the last street car to be used in East Toledo. Pictured above is Mayor Roy Start as he cut the tape at the end of the Starr Avenue line to start the car on its last trip. Looking on are Fred J. Young, head of the transportation committee of the East Toledo Club; Frank W. Wiley, president of the club, and Charles H. Forsgard, general manager of the CTC."

The last car in East Toledo on July 7, 1939, was CTC car No. 801, seen here on the Starr Avenue loop.

CTC cars No. 801 and No. 803 have just been delivered new to the Starr Avenue barn.

The Toledo Railfans Club rented CTC car No. 906 for $25 for a Sunday afternoon on October 25, 1945. Author Kirk F. Hise is standing in front of the car, which is stopped in front of the old Pennsylvania Railroad freight house on the sub track at Monroe and Summit Streets. This sub track was a place for the No. X1201 work car to park so that it would be handy in case of a trolley derailment or breakdown. The club toured the Cherry, Long Belt, and Nebraska routes with photograph opportunity stops en route.

This *c.* 1928 photograph from the CTC files shows an Overland factory shift change on Central Avenue west of the New York Central Railroad.

Here is the intersection of Summit Street at Adams Street. This *c.* 1928 photograph is from the CTC files.

The Starr Avenue carbarns are seen here in 1928. (Courtesy of the CTC files.)

The Central Avenue carbarns are seen in this 1928 photograph. (Courtesy of the CTC files.)

In this c. 1940 photograph, CTC car No. 810 is headed westbound on the Cherry Street bridge. This was one of the cars sold to Birmingham, Alabama, in 1942. (Courtesy of the W. E. Hague collection.)

This is the only known photograph (taken around 1916) of CTC car No. 811. The 800-series cars were built by Kuhlman Car Company of Cleveland in 1916. They were 50-foot steel cars, equipped with Thomlinson multiple unit couplers. They were delivered in pairs, running back to back. The No. 811 never made service in Toledo, as it was demolished in a railroad grade crossing accident at Central Avenue during delivery. In 1929, the multiple unit couplers were removed, and the changes in the car weight (400 pounds) resulted in a reduction in yearly power expenses.

In this photograph taken on June 30, 1948, the last Cherry Street car, CTC car No. 815, is seen on Tremainsville Road heading west to turn around and head back to Cherry Street. (Courtesy of the R. Hubbard collection.)

Here is another photograph of CTC car No. 815 leaving the wye on Tremainsville Road. It arrived at the Central Avenue barns at 7:30 p.m. on June, 30, 1948.

CTC car No. 826 is crossing New York Central tracks on Phillips Avenue in West Toledo in this c. 1940 photograph. A crossing watchman's shanty stood on the south side of the street, and a two-story tower stood on the north side at one time. (Courtesy of the Willard Edson collection.)

Nebraska car No. 828 is leaving the end-of-the-line loop at Brown Avenue and Nebraska Avenue in this photograph taken on September 20, 1947. (Courtesy of the W. E. Hague collection.)

CTC car No. 830 turns on the Lagrange Street loop at Manhattan Boulevard in this *c.* 1938 photograph. (Courtesy of the H. Haack collection.)

CTC car No. 833 of the Nebraska line had an eclipse fender and original coupler, as seen in this *c.* 1919 photograph. (Courtesy of the Kirk F. Hise collection.)

CTC car No. 736 was rebuilt from the 500-series cars. It is seen here on Summit Street just south of Monroe Street. (Courtesy of the CTC files.)

CTC car No. 738 is seen here around 1940 in the scrap lines at the Central Avenue barns. (Courtesy of the H. Haack collection.)

CTC car No. 834 turns on the Starr Avenue loop near Toledo Terminal Railroad. Labor Day 1939 saw the completion of the $1 million Central Avenue subway beneath the Michigan Central Railroad tracks, replacing the former grade crossing that took many lives. E. L. Graumlich, street railway commissioner, boasted that the Long Belt line would be one of the finest in the city. The cars detoured over Nestlewood Avenue, where a temporary crossing was built over the railroad. In order to make the detour, the city had to acquire property on which three houses were located. The houses were moved, and a street was paved from Central to Nestlewood Avenues at Maple Avenue. Another piece of property at Albion Street was acquired to enable the continuance of Nestlewood Avenue over the railroad track, and another building had to be moved. This photograph was taken around 1939. (Courtesy of the CTC files.)

Two CTC 800-series cars are pictured around 1943 at the Cherry Street line wye at Old Point in West Toledo. The wye was used by Toledo city cars and the T&W to turn cars back on their routes. The T&W in later years did not run downtown and turned here. The Cherry Street line terminated here, until 1923, when it was extended out Sylvania Avenue and along Tremainsville Road to a wye at the Toledo Terminal Railroad. The T&W track had been on the south side of Sylvania Avenue. The new double track was laid in the middle of Sylvania Avenue and replaced the T&W service along here. Although the rail remained in the pavement until the end of trolleys on the Cherry Street line, the trolley wire was removed. (Courtesy of the Willard Edson collection.)

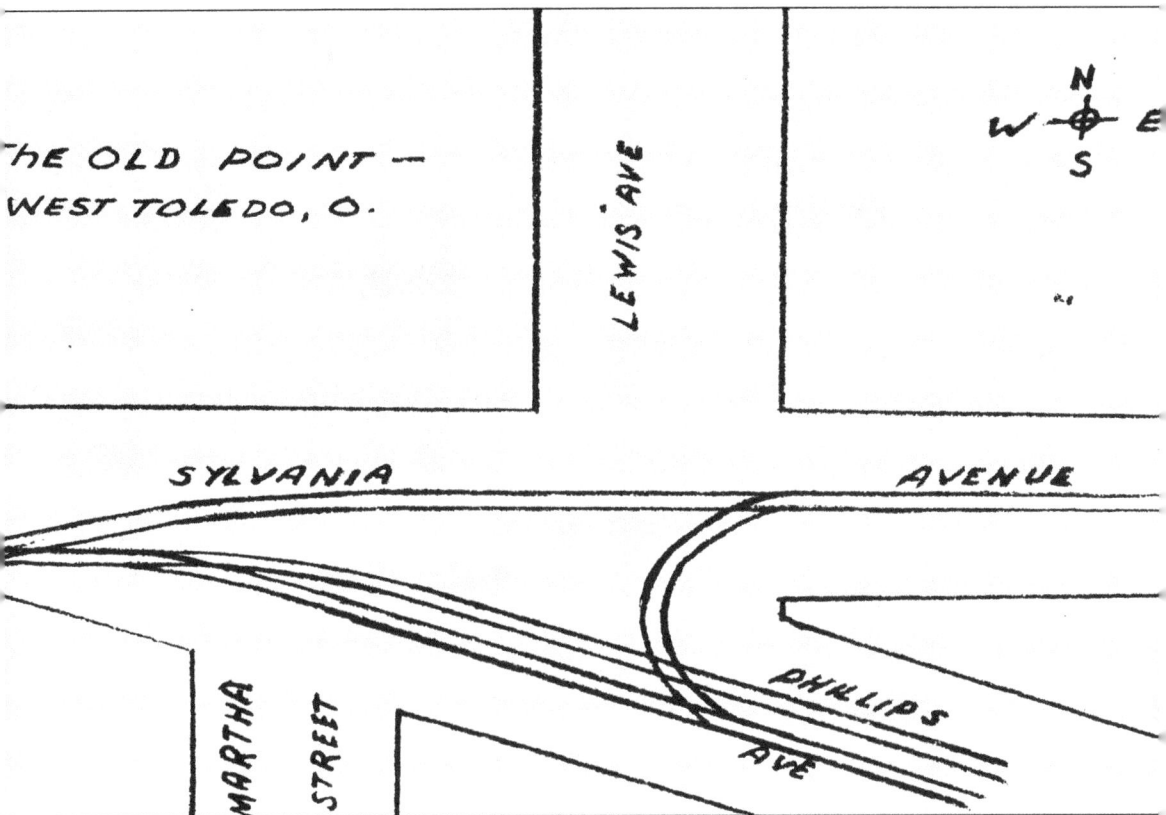

THE OLD POINT —
WEST TOLEDO, O.

LEWIS AVE

SYLVANIA AVENUE

MARTHA STREET

PHILLIPS AVE

N
W E
S

The wye at the end for the Cherry line on Tremainsville Road was used until the end of trolley service. The motorman headed his car into the north leg of the wye, over the second switch. He would close the controller and go to the rear of the car and open the center end window. There was a small switch box under the window with one notch on the controller. An air brake handle and a reverser handle were needed there also to control the reversing of the car.

CTC car No. 835 is pictured here around 1946 at the wye turnaround on Tremainsville Road at the end of the Cherry Street line.

Toledo railfans chartered a trip on CTC car No. 906, seen here in the wye on Tremainsville Road, and car No. 835, a regular Cherry Street car, on October, 28, 1945.

This CTC car No. 838 was refurbished in 1928 and still retains rattan seats and a heating stove at the front of the car by the motorman. The conductor was positioned at the center doors with the fare box near the entrance car and front exit. There was no honor system here for fare payment. This photograph was taken around 1928.

This *c.* 1928 photograph shows the rear interior of CTC car No. 838.

The front interior of CTC car No. 838 is seen in this *c.* 1928 photograph.

Sporting a very new paint job, CTC car No. 839 sits at the Central Avenue barns in this *c.* 1946 photograph. (Courtesy of the H. Haack collection.)

On August 1, 1937, W. E. Hague took this photograph of CTC car No. 841 from the Toledo-bound LSE car that is at the end-of-the-line loop on Woodville Road at Pickle Road. The destination sign reads, "Starr Avenue on next outbound trip car will run on Starr Line." (Courtesy of the W. E. Hague collection.)

This trolley, CTC car No. 843, heads west for the barns on Central Avenue. After finishing their runs in the evening, Cherry Street cars inbound from West Toledo would turn west on Central Avenue to go to the Central Avenue carbarns. Author Kirk F. Hise was allowed to stay on for the ride off Cherry Street a few times on the single track on Central Avenue across Collingwood Avenue, back on a double track, and to the barns. Then he would catch a Long Belt line car in either direction to downtown and back on a Cherry Street car or a bus back to West Toledo. The Cherry Street crosstown line used this track until June 10, 1920. It is unknown how far this line was operated. This photograph was taken around 1944.

Seen in this c. 1929 photograph, this 800-series car ran in November 1929, advertising an industrial exposition at the building that now houses the Erie Street Market. (Courtesy of the CTC files.)

CTC car No. 845 is seen in this c. 1945 photograph on Detroit Avenue near Phillips Avenue, crossing over temporary track work. (Courtesy of the Willard Edson collection.)

CTC car No. 849 was equipped with a coal stove and original couplers. It is seen here around 1927 at the Starr Avenue barn. (Courtesy of the Kirk F. Hise collection.)

CTC car No. 849 snagged its kite in rush-hour traffic. Car No. 858 is coming to the rescue in this c. 1945 photograph. (Courtesy of the Willard Edson collection.)

There is an advertisement to join the Navy Seabees on CTC car No. 850 on Cherry Street in this *c.* 1944 photograph. (Courtesy of the Willard Edson collection.)

The Park Theatre is located on the left in this *c.* 1947 photograph, and the Bib and Tucker restaurant is behind CTC car No. 854 at Old Point in West Toledo. Also, the wye track can still be seen in the street. The 800s had double center doors on one side of the car. As they were one-man operated, the doors were exit only and were opened by standing on a treadle on the car floor. The motorman had no control over their operation. (Courtesy of the H. Haack collection.)

Old Flower Hospital can be seen in the background of this *c.* 1942 photograph of CTC car No. 854 on the Cherry line at Manhattan Boulevard and Collingwood Avenue. The Cherry Street line ran past Central Catholic High School. When students got out of school, they would ride the streetcars home. A number of students would wait at the car stop, and when a car stopped, one would get on the trolley, pay his fare, and run back to the center doors and stand on the floor treadle to open them. The car could not be moved as long as the doors were opened, and a lot of students would climb aboard for a free ride. The CTC finally had to put an inspector on the cars at schooltime to put a stop to this practice. (Courtesy of the Willard Edson collection.)

The Union Depot line ran from Madison Avenue to Summit Street to Knapp Street to the Union Depot and back. CTC car No. 904 is seen on the Union Station route in this *c.* 1939 photograph.

CTC car No. 904 is pictured in this *c.* 1946 photograph at the carbarns on Central Avenue. (Courtesy of the Kirk F. Hise collection.)

The end of the Stickney line is seen here around 1939 with CTC car No. 905. The line had been cut back to Manhattan Boulevard. It ran from Adams Street to Superior Street south on Jefferson Avenue to Summit Street to Adams Street, passing the courthouse to Michigan Street. It went out Michigan to Canton Avenue to Cherry Street to Sherman Street, then east to Forest Cemetery and north on Stickney Avenue, and out Stickney across Manhattan Boulevard to Elbon Street just around here on the west side of Stickney. The old Toledo Airport was a short way north of the Michigan Central Railroad. The Detroit, Monroe and Toledo Short Line entered Toledo over the Stickney line. (Courtesy of the F. D. Cairns collection.)

Seen here in front of the carbarns on Central Avenue around 1945 is CTC car No. 802 with a fresh paint job. (Courtesy of the H. Haack collection.)

A 900-series Long Belt car on Adams Street is in this *c.* 1945 photograph. (Courtesy of the Kirk F. Hise collection.)

The Toledo Railfans Club toured the three remaining trolley lines on Sunday, October 28, 1945. They chartered CTC car No. 906, seen here at the end of the Cherry Street line wye along Tremainsville Road in this *c.* 1945 photograph. (Courtesy of the W. E. Hague collection.)

This building was originally a streetcar barn and later became the old Pennsylvania Railroad freight house. The chartered CTC car No. 906 is on the stub track at Summit and Monroe Streets in this c. 1945 photograph. (Courtesy of the Willard Edson collection.)

Seen in this c. 1910 photograph, TRY&L car No. 999 was an express car on Summit Street. This car was 46 feet long and had a wood body. It was used as a freight car on Maumee Valley until the end of service on March 3, 1920, and was renumbered as X-1103.

TRY&L car No. 601 is seen here around 1905 crossing the Maumee River to Maumee on the Maumee Valley line. (Courtesy of the F. D. Cairns collection.)

This c. 1945 photograph of CTC car No. 906 was taken at the end-of-the-line loop on Nebraska Avenue at Brown Avenue. The 900-series cars were built by Perley-Thomas Company of Durham, South Carolina, in 1923. The CTC purchased eight cars on June 4, 1931. They were double-ended cars, 39 feet long with 44 seats. They could have been used on some routes such as Stickney Avenue, which had been cut back and did not require turning at the end of the line. Being smaller than the 800s, they were used more often as spare or extra cars during later years of CTC trolleys. They were cut up, burned, and scrapped at the Central Avenue barns after trolley operation ceased in 1950. (Courtesy of the F. D. Cairns collection.)

The body of car No. 837 was being used as a home on Whiteford Road, south of Alexis Road, as seen in this *c.* 1963 photograph. This was one of two car bodies there were sold in 1950. (Courtesy of the Kirk F. Hise collection.)

Birmingham Electric Company car No. 427 was originally used by the CTC and is seen in this *c.* 1942 photograph at the carbarns in Birmingham. The CTC sold 23 No. 800s to the Birmingham Electric Company in 1941. (Courtesy of Korkes Photograph.)

CTC car No. 908 is being scrapped at the Central Avenue carbarns in this c. 1950 photograph. (Courtesy of the H. Haack collection.)

Two

PRIVATE CAR TOLEDO

The private car Toledo is seen here at the Central Avenue barns around 1938. "The special car 'Toledo' will be put into service between this city and Cleveland to carry the groups attending the meeting. It will leave here each day about 6 am and return late in the evening. E.L. Graumlich, street railway commissioner; J. Frank Johnson, vice president and general manager; C.H. Forsgard, general superintendent; H.R. Roudebush, secretary-treasurer and auditor, and Don Finkbeiner, claims attorney, of the CTC will attend most of the sessions. During the week, 25 men of the supervisory forces of the company with all of the winning captains and high men in the safety contests of the company will be guests at the convention."

As car lines were abandoned and converted to bus operations, some cars became excess. In 1942, 23 of the 800s were sold to Birmingham, Alabama, for wartime use. They ran out their days there. In 1949, the last car line in Toledo, the Long Belt line, was abandoned, and all remaining cars were scrapped at the Central Avenue carbarns. Two car bodies were sold, and they are now gone. The private car Toledo survives at Trolleyville USA, a trolley museum near Cleveland, and car No. 582 is at the Northern Ohio Trolley Museum near Chippewa Lake. Tarta replaced the CTC in 1971, and it continues bus transportation today on many routes that began in the trolley days. This photograph shows an interior shot of the Toledo.

Here is another photograph showing the interior of the Toledo, built by TRY&L in 1906. It was 48 feet, 2 inches long and had chairs for 22 persons. After retirement, it first went to Lake Shore Electric Lake Park at Sages Grove, east of Vermillion on Lake Erie. It is now at Trolleyville USA.

The private car Toledo is pictured here around 1940 at Sages Grove, which was a summer vacation park for a number of years. The second car is TRY&L car No. 582. The final car is a Sandusky City car. (Courtesy of the W. McCallab collection.)

Three

MAINTENANCE OF WAY AND OTHER EQUIPMENT

CTC car No. 1006 is a snow sweeper pictured here in the yard at the Central Avenue barns around 1946. (Courtesy of the Kirk F. Hise collection.)

This snow sweeper, CTC car No. X1011, was built by McGuire Cummings Car Company in 1914. This photograph was taken around 1944. (Courtesy of the H. Haack collection.)

Pay car No. 1015 was rebuilt into sand car No. X1105 by TRY&L in 1907. (Courtesy of the J. Lusk collection.)

CTC car No. X1104 is a sand car and is pictured here around 1940 at the Central Avenue barns. Its old number was No. 1010, but it was rebuilt by TRY&L in 1905. This car was 24 feet long. (Courtesy of the H. Haack collection.)

Originally numbered 1041 and built by TRY&L, this CTC No. X1201 crane car is taking the crossing on Nebraska Avenue at the Michigan Central Belt Railway. This photograph was taken around 1945. (Courtesy of the W. E. Hague collection.)

CTC car No. X1201 sits at the Central Avenue barns around 1940. (Courtesy of the H. Haack collection.)

Also sitting at the Central Avenue carbarns is CTC car No. X1202 in this *c.* 1940 photograph.

This *c.* 1928 photograph shows CTC car No. X1202 after it was rebuilt. (Courtesy of the CTC files.)

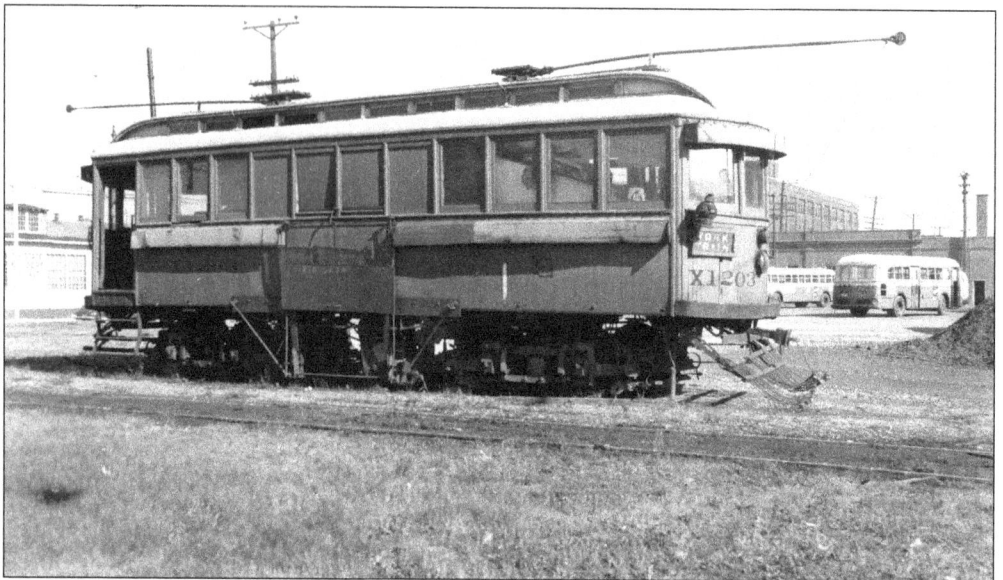

Car No. 1040 was built by TRY&L in 1903 but was later wrecked. CTC car No. X1203 was a rail grinder at the Central Avenue barns. Later it was rebuilt by the CTC as a rail grinder for the cost of $4,208.33 and was renumbered X1203. This photograph was taken around 1944. (Courtesy of the F. D. Cairns collection.)

The CTC car No. X1203 rail grinder is seen here at work at the end of the Nebraska line in this c. 1946 photograph. (Courtesy of the W. E. Hague collection.)

CTC car No. X1207 is seen here at the Central Avenue barns around 1945. (Courtesy of the F. D. Cairns collection.)

A differential locomotive dump car, CTC car No. X1207, is seen here at the Toledo Edison Acme plant in East Toledo. After trolley abandonment, this car was sold to the Toledo Edison. It was never used there and was eventually scrapped. This locomotive was built on September 16, 1922, by the Findlay Car Company.

CTC car No. X1208, a differential dump car, was built in Findlay in 1922. This c. 1940 photograph was taken at the Central Avenue carbarns. (Courtesy of the H. Haack collection.)

Four

INTERURBANS IN TOLEDO

1. Lake Shore Electric
2. Ohio Electric, Lima-Toledo, Cincinnati & Lake Erie
3. Toledo & Indiana
4. Toledo & Maumee Valley
5. Toledo& Monroe, Detroit, Monroe & Toledo Short Line, Detroit United and Eastern Michigan-Toledo
6. Toledo & Point Place Interurban
7. Toledo & Western
8. Toledo & Bowling Green & Southern
9. Toledo, Fostoria & Findlay
10. Toledo, Ottawa Beach & Northern
11. Toledo, Pt. Clinton & Lakeside, Northwestern Ohio Railway & Power, Ohio Public Service and Toledo & Eastern

This list shows all the interurban lines that were once operating in Toledo.

The first interurban station in Toledo was at the corner of Summit and Orange Streets. The cars paused at the corner, staying on Summit Street, then proceeded on a loop south to Monroe Street and back to Superior Street to Cherry Street and then east or west and north on their own routes. The Ohio Electric had its own station at Avondale and Eleventh Streets, because the cars were too long to make the sharp turns of the city streetcar lines. After 1902, a large station opened in the Smith and Baker Building on Superior Street at Jefferson Avenue. This was at 339 Superior Street on the west side of the street, so cars made the trip south on Superior Street and then returned via Monroe and Summit Streets. In 1909, the depot was moved to the 500 block of Superior Street near Jackson Avenue. This was on the east side of the street, and the loop was reversed and remained at this location until the last interurban, the OPS, made the last stop on July 11, 1939. This photograph was taken on March 8, 1987. (Courtesy of the Willard Edson collection.)

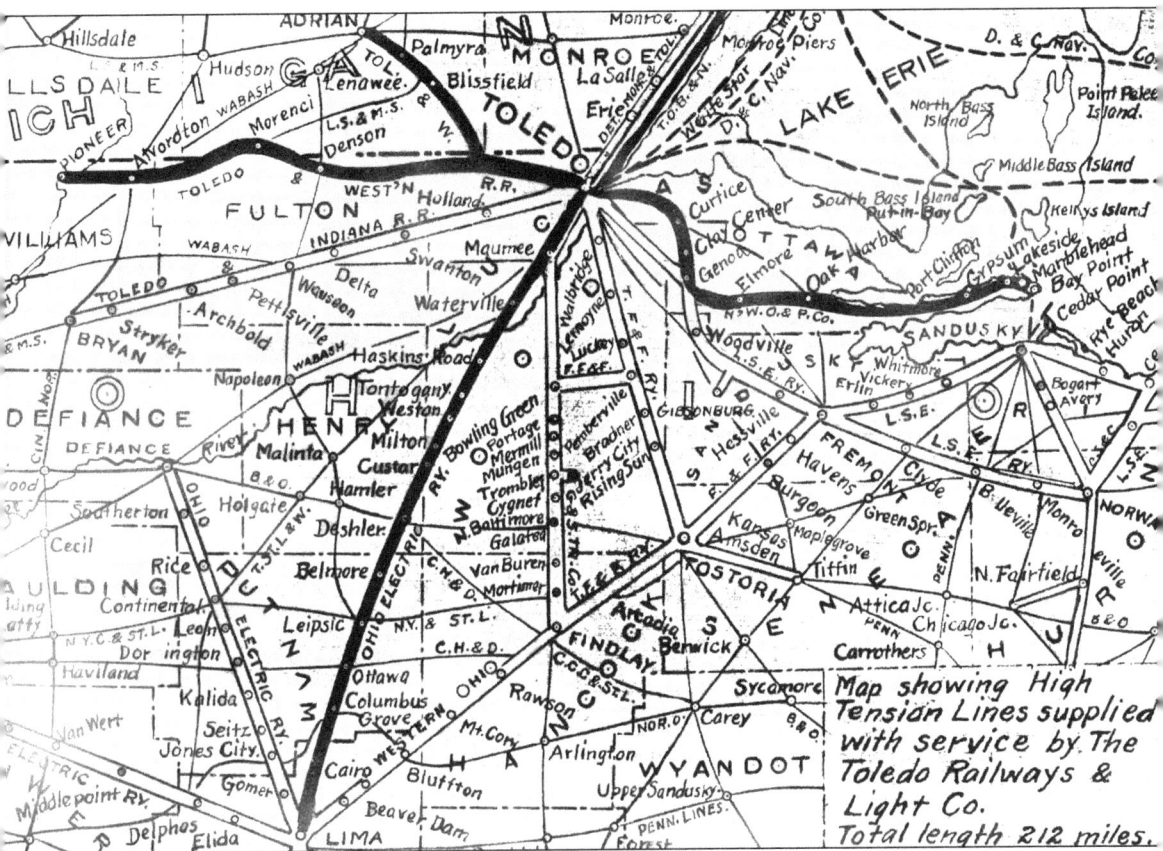

This map shows all the interurban lines that serviced Toledo.

LSE car No. 182 is seen here at Toledo Interurban Station. (Courtesy of the P. Jenks collection.)

In this c. 1935 photograph, LSE car No. 31 sits at the Glendale freight yards on Woodville Road, west of the Toledo Terminal Railroad in East Toledo.

This c. 1938 photograph shows the LSE at the Cincinnati and Lake Erie (C&LE) station on Lafayette Street. The LSE cars used to lay over here between trips. (Courtesy of the H. Haack collection.)

Ohio Electric Railway transit freight trailers are being loaded at the LSE Glendale freight yards on Woodville Road in this c. 1931 photograph. These yards were just west of the Toledo Terminal Railroad. The trailers were run up a small ramp, then a flatcar would be pushed underneath them, and they were tied down for transit. (Courtesy of the F. D. Cairns collection.)

LSE substation Hayes was located in Toledo on Woodville Road in this *c*. 1936 photograph.

Here is another *c*. 1936 photograph of the Hayes substation after the tracks were removed.

This LSE car is on Woodville Road at Groll Road, now near Great Eastern Shopping Center, in this *c.* 1902 photograph. (Courtesy of the Bob Lorenz collection.)

The Ohio Electric–Toledo Terminal viaduct in South Toledo near Gould Tower is seen here. Bowser High School is near this right-of-way.

The Ohio Electric tunnel under Detroit Avenue is seen here around 1908. This concrete work is still in place.

Both c. 1958 photographs show the C&LE tunnel under Detroit Avenue in South Toledo by Bowser High School. (Courtesy of the Kirk F. Hise collection.)

The Ohio Electric, later C&LE, station is seen here on Lafayette Street around 1940. (Courtesy of the Willard Edson collection.)

The Lafayette station is seen here from another view.

The C&LE freight house on Lafayette Street is seen here around 1938 after abandonment. (Courtesy of the H. Haack collection.)

Ohio Electric car No. 182 sits at the Lafayette Street station.

This c. 1974 view of the Toledo and Indiana Railroad (T&I) freight house from Washington Street looks north. This building is now used as Fireman's Union Hall. (Courtesy the Kirk F. Hise collection.)

T&I car No. 53 is located here at Vulcan Tower at Dorr Street and Westwood Avenue around 1934.

One of the T&I cars built by Cincinnati Car Company in 1924, car No. 110 is pictured here at Dorr Street station around 1948. After abandonment, they were sold to Atlanta Power Company. (Courtesy of the H. Haack collection.)

T&I car No. 54 freight motorcar, which had been No. 80 on the T&W is seen here. This photograph was taken at Vulcan station on Dorr Street. Vulcan Tower is in the background, and the Toledo Terminal water tank for locomotives is shown around 1938. (Courtesy of the Dr. S. King collection.)

Toledo and Maumee Valley car No. 25 had earlier carried a single-digit number and was painted blue. When the Maumee Valley came under Everett-Moore Syndicate control, the cars were renumbered and painted yellow in about 1910. This photograph was taken around 1900.

Toledo and Maumee Valley car No. 503 sits in front of the carbarn at Perrysburg on Indiana Avenue at East Boundary Street in this c. 1905 photograph.

A Maumee Valley and Light car sits at the Perrysburg carbarn at East Boundary Street and Indiana Avenue. Cincinnati Car Company built seven of these cars for the Maumee Valley line in 1922. When the Maumee Valley abandoned in 1927, they were returned to the car builder and sold to the Cincinnati Street Railway. They ran there until abandonment of the Cincinnati system. (Courtesy of the R. Hubbard collection.)

Bowling green Bridge
maumee. O.

This c. 1908 photograph of the Toledo and Maumee Valley and Toledo, Bowling Green and Southern bridge looks toward Maumee.

Toledo & Maumee Valley Ry.
oledo, Bowling Green & Fremont Ry.

THE LONGEST ELECTRIC BELT LINE IN THE UNITED STATES.

LEAGE { T. & M. V. Ry .... 22 miles.
{ T. B. G. & F. Ry. (owned and leased lines)...... 38 „
        Total mileage............................ 60 miles.

nning through the famous Indian Battle Fields. passing ort Meigs and Fort Miami, and near Turkey Foot Rock.

s leave Toledo for Maumee and Perrysburg every 28 minutes. Time for round trip, 1 hour and 52 minutes.
s leave Toledo for Bowling Green (28 miles) every 56 minutes. Time for round trip, 3 hours.
ourists at Put-In-Bay and those going east or west will be amply re- d by stopping at Toledo for a trip over this famous and beautiful route.

K. DETWILER, President T. & M. V. Ry. H. WALBRIDGE, President T. B. G. & F. Ry.	C. A. DENMAN, Gen. Manager. . B. BROCKWAY Auditor. General Offices — Toledo, O.

This is a *c.* 1898 newspaper advertisement for the Toledo and Maumee Valley Railway and the Toledo, Bowling Green and Fremont Railway.

Detroit, Monroe and Toledo car No. 7518 is pictured here around 1910 along Stickney Avenue south of the Ottawa River trestle north of Toledo. (Courtesy of the Kirk F. Hise collection.)

The Detroit, Monroe and Toledo gang and section men work on the replacement bridge over the Ottawa River along Stickney Avenue. Toussant Jacobs is second from the right in the front row. Later he worked as a section man on the Pere Marquette Railroad at Erie. Work motorcar No. 7605 is in the background of this c. 1956 photograph.

This is the Detroit, Monroe and Toledo Short Line car No. 506 at Toledo Interurban Station in downtown Toledo around 1910. (Courtesy of the W. E. Hague collection.)

This car, Detroit United Railway car No. 7526 at the interurban station in Toledo, was called Menominee and ran many times over the LSE to Cleveland. This photograph was taken around 1928.

Pictured here at an unknown location crossing a bridge is car No. 429 on the Point Place line. The car was built by the J. G. Brill Company in 1901 and had a capacity of 40 seats.

Behind the boat is TRY&L car No. 429 at the end of the Point Place on Edgewater Drive. The postcard is dated January 4, 1912.

This is the T&W freight house station on Sylvania Avenue in West Toledo. This *c.* 1903 photograph is from the company files.

Pictured here with the flag flying high is the T&W storefront station at Trilby. (Courtesy of the Dr. M. Camp collection.)

Pictured here is T&W car No. 404 in West Toledo on Tremainsville Road west of the Toledo Terminal Railroad. This was the location of the loading used for the Willys-Overland cars from the factory.

Workers relax on T&W engine No. 404.

Pictured here around 1937 is the T&W right-of-way looking east along Tremainsville Road during abandonment, as plainly seen by the overgrown tracks. (Courtesy of the H. Haack collection.)

The Sylvania carbarns for the T&W, pictured here, is now the location of a supermarket.

T&W car No. 403 heads westbound, crossing Monroe Street in Sylvania with a string of boxcars loaded with Willys-Overland automobiles in this *c.* 1930 photograph. (Courtesy of the Joe Galloway collection.)

T&W car No. 21 was a lightweight car built by Cincinnati Car Company in 1921. These cars served the T&W until abandonment in 1937. It then served as a diner called White City on Route 20 south of Lyons and burned in 1995.

The Sylvania carbarn can be seen in the background of this *c.* 1931 photograph of T&W car No. 61. Car No. 61 had a rail postal office section, and mail was sorted en route. (Courtesy of the Joe Galloway collection.)

T&W car No. 50 is seen here around 1907 at Allen Junction west of Sylvania on the wye headed north toward Adrian. (Courtesy of the F. D. Cairns collection.)

The Toledo & Western Railroad Co.

RECEIPT FOR ONE WAY FARE

This receipt when properly punched, is good for one continuous ride between Stations so designated, on this date and train only. Conductors will punch the amount of fare paid.

President & Gen'l Mgr

1909 1910 1911 1912 1913 1914 1915

JAN FEB MAR APR MAY JUN | JUL AUG SEP OCT NOV DEC
DAY 17 18 19 20 21 22 23 24 25 26 27 28 29 30 31
1 2 3 4 5 6 7 8 9 10 11 12 13 14 15 16

HALF O FARE

Station	Fare
Harris Place	02
Wernert	03
Cresceus	
Whiteford Road	04
Centennial	
SYLVANIA	05
Smith's Siding	06
Allen Junction	
Bowen	07
BERKEY	
County Line	08
METAMORA	09
Champion	
White ville	10
Town Line	
Seward	15
LYONS	20
Beebe	
Denson	25
Ranger	
MORENCI	30
Wolcott	
Powers	35
Handy Corners	
FAYETTE	40
Gorham	45
Mill Creek	
Franklin	50
ALVORDTON	
Madison	55
Throne	
PIONEER	60
Southland	65
Korth	70
Holtz	75
Tag sold	
RIGA	80
BLISS FIELD	
Harrison	85
PALMYRA	
Clark	90
Nash	95
Wabash Subway	
ADRIAN	$1

This ticket was for the T&W and was good to Fayette, as seen by the punch hole over Fayette.

This is the c. 1901 builder's photograph at Cincinnati Car Company of Toledo, Bowling Green and Southern car No. 160. (Courtesy of the Kirk F. Hise collection.)

Toledo, Bowling Green and Southern car No. 205 is seen here around 1925 at the Toledo Interurban Station. (Courtesy of the Joe Galloway collection.)

Pictured in this *c.* 1925 photograph is Toledo, Bowling Green and Southern car No. 315 at the Toledo freight station on South Erie Street.

This Toledo, Bowling Green and Southern car sits alongside the Dixie Highway south of Perrysburg. This *c.* 1928 photograph was taken from a moving Model T by F. D. Cairns. (Courtesy of the F. D. Cairns collection.)

This is the Toledo, Bowling Green and Southern freight house on South St. Clair Street around 1974. (Courtesy of the Kirk F. Hise collection.)

Pictured here is the Toledo, Bowling Green and Southern bridge over the Maumee River between Maumee and Perrysburg. The postcard is dated 1923. The piers are still standing.

This TF&F car is in the subway under the New York Central Railroad near Vickers Tower, crossing the Toledo Terminal lines by Drouillard Road. The TF&F followed the Bay Terminal Railroad from Woodville Road. (Courtesy of the Kirk F. Hise collection.)

TF&F car No. 19 is pictured here at Walbridge station. The postcard is dated April 26, 1929. This is the closest photograph of a TF&F car near Toledo that the authors have.

Pictured in this *c.* 1908 photograph is the TF&F car No. 11 built by Jewett Car Company. (Courtesy of the F. D. Cairns collection.)

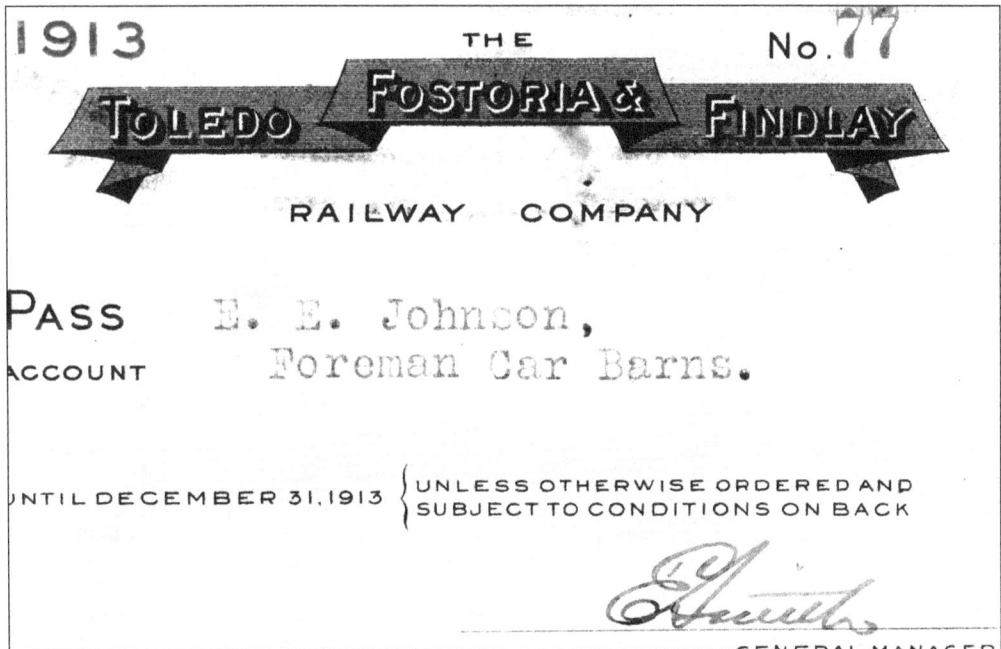

Railway passes have changed greatly since this one for the TF&F, for E. E. Johnson in 1913.

Pictured here is CTC car No. 444 in Michigan on the last trip south of the Toledo Beach line on October 17, 1927. (Courtesy of the F. D. Cairns collection.)

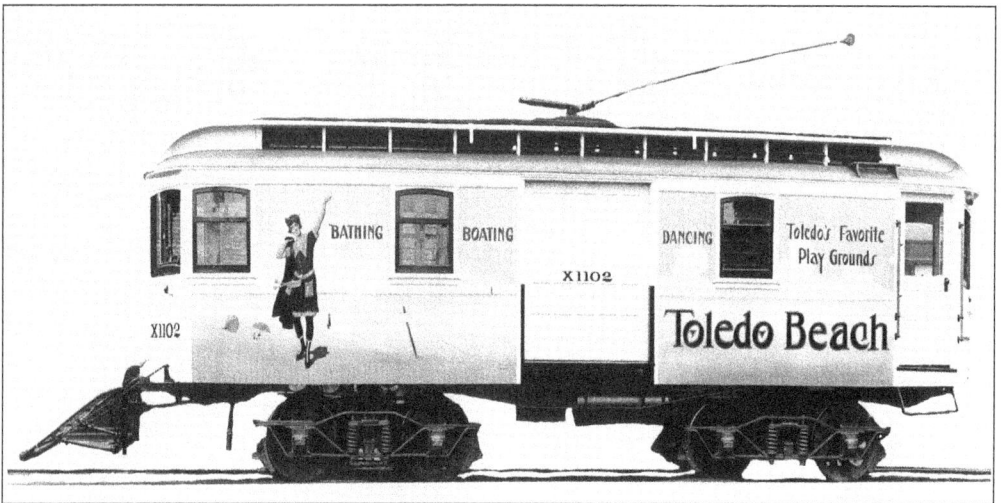

The Toledo Beach line had an express car painted white on the sides, on which was painted a bathing suit beauty of the day. The rest was used to advertise the features of the beach. The car was numbered 998 and later was changed to X1102. The car had been built by TRY&L in 1906.

122

This Toledo, Ottawa Beach and Northern Railway Company ticket appears to have never been used.

The Toledo, Ottawa Beach & Northern Railway Company ticket

H			88681

	TO	FROM
	CAS INO	
10	SCHOOL HOUSE	
	OTTAWA R IVER ROAD	
	DUSSEA U ROAD	
15	GRAND TR UNK SDG.	
	ERIE ROAD	
20	LAKE SIDE	
	TOLEDO BEACH	
	POINT PLACE	
	DO G	
FARE PAID	BAGG A G E	
	HALF FARE	

AUDITOR'S CHECK

NOT GOOD FOR TRANSPORTATION.

TO BE SENT TO AUDITOR WITH CONDUCTOR'S TRIP REPORT.

TOLEDO BEACH

Renowned as

The Most Beautiful Resort on the Lakes . . . .

BATHING

Along a Four Mile Stretch of Sand

"The Atlantic City of the West"

Your visit to Toledo is incomplete if you

miss a Trolley Trip to

TOLEDO   BEACH

A 17 Mile Ride Absolutely Unsurpassed for Scenic Beauty

This advertisement encouraged people to get to Toledo Beach by using the trolley. It was printed in *Yachting Calendar* for 1909.

This postcard shows a trolley full of passengers heading for Toledo Beach. The date of publication is unknown.

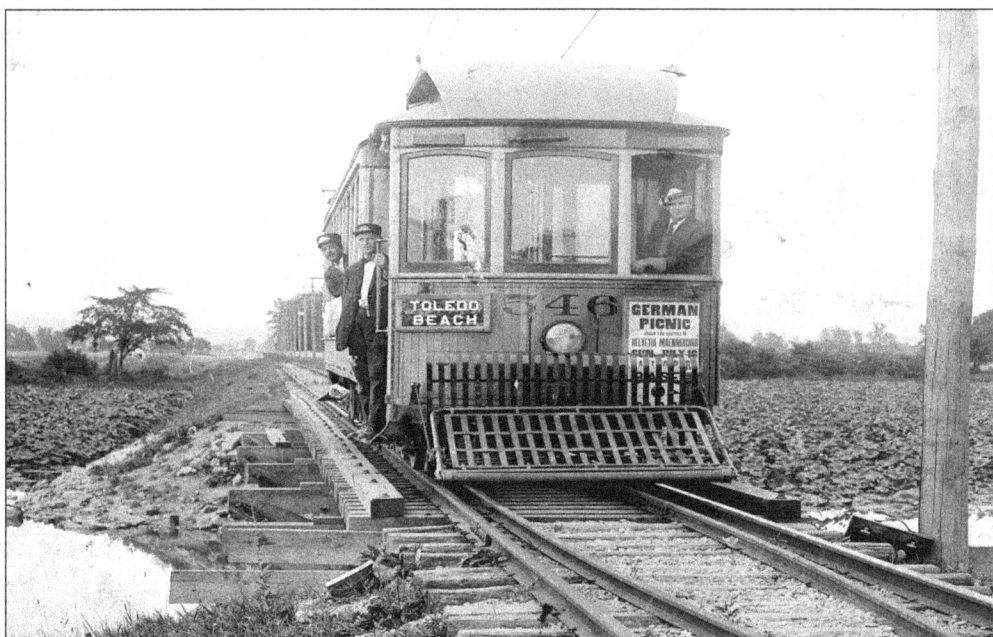

This is another view of the Toledo Beach trolley. Note the poster on the front of the car advertising a German picnic. The date of publication is unknown.

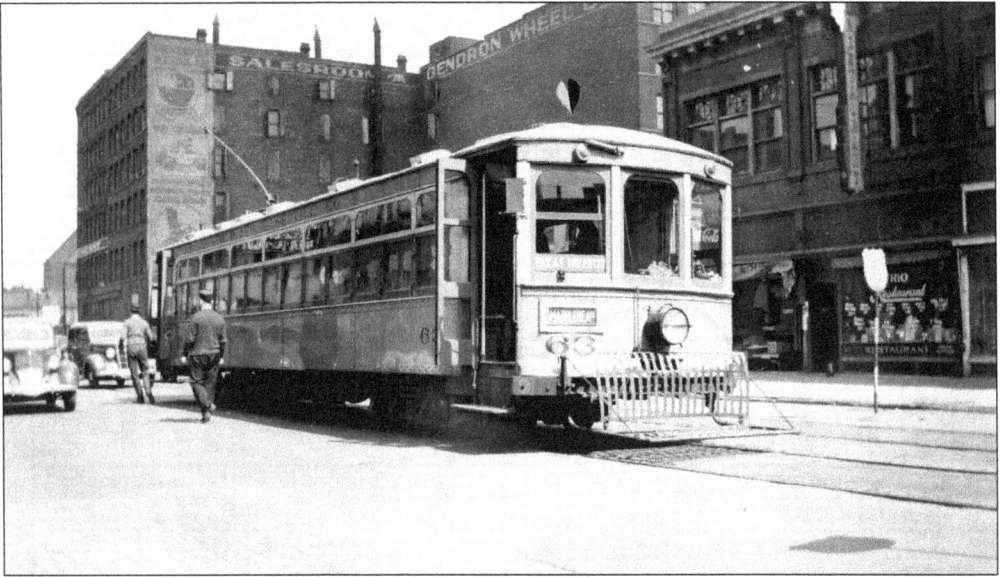

This *c.* 1937 photograph shows OPS car No. 63 at the Toledo Interurban Station.

This is OPS car No. 321 at the Toledo Interurban Station at Superior and Jackson Streets, during a railfan trip. This photograph was taken around 1939.

THE OHIO PUBLIC SERVICE COMPANY

Passenger's Receipt for Fare Paid From and To Stations Punched.
Good only for continuous passage, for train and day punched.
PASSENGER TO RETAIN THIS RECEIPT AS EVIDENCE OF FARE PAID.

Div. Mgr.

No. 877531

This is an unused OPS ticket.

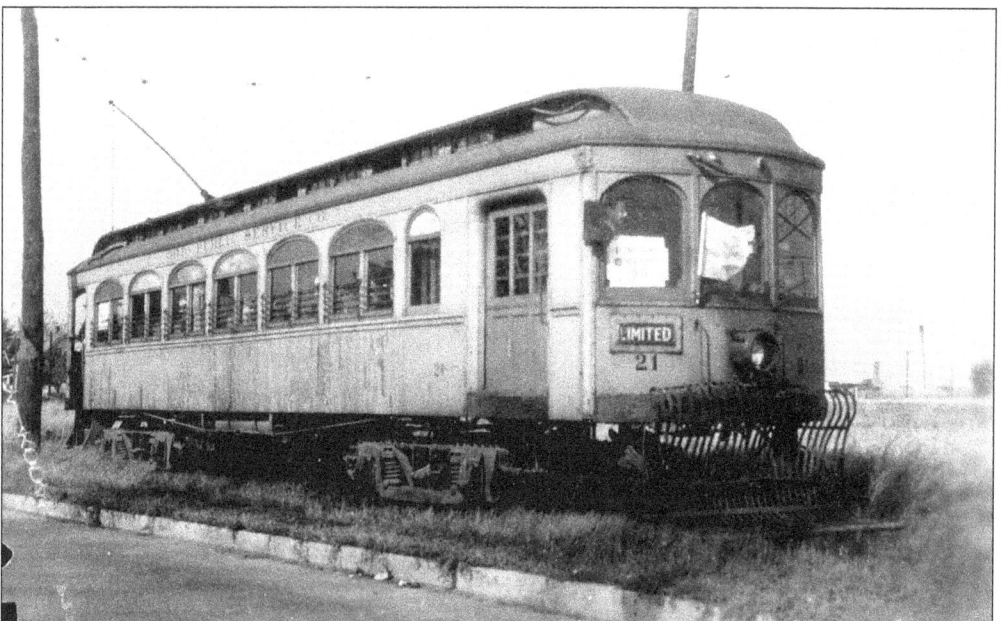

Pictured here is OPS car No. 21 on a National Railroad Historical Society fan trip in 1939. The photograph was taken on the east side of Toledo Terminal at the crossing on Starr Avenue. This crossing was protected by derailed switched, and sometimes cars were derailed here.

Pictured here is the Toledo and Eastern at Ryan station, at the Starr Avenue and Toledo Terminal Railroad connection. (Courtesy of the Bob Lorenz collection.)

This is the OPS at Ryan station at the Starr Avenue and Toledo Terminal Railroad interchange of the Toledo and Eastern. This photograph was taken around 1950. (Courtesy of the F. D. Cairns collection.)

Visit us at
arcadiapublishing.com

....

www.ingramcontent.com/pod-product-compliance
Lightning Source LLC
Chambersburg PA
CBHW050602110426
42813CB00008B/2440